NONNA AND MADDOX

A Day In the Life Of An Ordinary Boy

Author **Lynette Spano**
Co-Author **Maddox Karpeshov**

My name is Maddox, I am 6 years old
and I live with my nonna.
(That's grandmother in Italian.)

Families come in different shapes and sizes.
My Mommy is in school and daddy is building a business.
They love me but they can't take care of me right now.
So I live with Nonna

My nonna tells me stories
about living in Italy. Her first Love
was Rome until I was born.

My life is like any ordinary kid.
My nonna comes into my room every morning and says, "Wake up sleepy head!"
POWER

Then she says "Maddox go brush your teeth!"
Nonna taught me a song. "Up and down,
brush your teeth, clean them side by side,
up and down." I sing and hum while I brush
my teeth.

Nonna says, "Come eat your breakfast.
We have to leave soon for school."

"Hurry up grab your bookbag!" she says.
And, I rush to the sofa and get my bag
as Nonna is leaving to walk me to school.

When I come home, I have to do homework.
My nonna helps me with my math, reading
and writing my letters .

My nonna and I are a team. We go grocery shopping.
I like to pick mostly cookies and marshmallow and candy,
Nonna picks the eggs and says, "Hey, buddy, to much candy!"
I laugh.

I also go to Taekwondo every week.
I just won a trophy at my first competition.
I ask, "Nonna are you proud of me?"
She says, "Absolutely, my love. You're my star!"

Nonna says I have to learn how to swim in case
I fall out of a boat and into the ocean.
After my lesson, we stay and swim together in the pool.

Nonna talks about being helpful and sharing in the care of our home like...

...sweeping the floor,

cleaning,

and doing the dishes.

I have lots of chores. Clean my room, put my clothes away...

feed my cat, feed my fish.

Sometimes I have a tantru
and Nonna has to give me a time ou
She reads a book called 123 Magic. After she's done, she says
"Maddox that's 1", if I go on with the tantrum she say
"Maddox that's 2" finally if I don't stop she say
"That's 3! "Take a 6 minute time ou
She reads in the book,
timing one minute for every year old I am
I'm six, so I have a six-minute time out.
I'm not happy. Huff.

After my time out, she says "Ok, time out Over!"
Then she hugs me and gives me a great big kiss.

Nona told about how we all have love buckets
and they are either full or empty or low.
When I do something that's naughty and
I get a time out my love bucket is really low,
or if I had a bad day my love bucket would be really low.

But, when my grandma Nona hugs me and runs her hands through my hair, my love bucket is really filled.
She asked "SO how's your love bucket honey?"
I say "Far high above the clouds."

Nonna says It's important to play together,
so we always make time for playing.

I try to get Nona to ride my scooter.
It's really funny to watch her trying,
but I get scared she might fall.

Nonna's knee was hurting, so she went to the doctor.
They said she needs a knee operation to make it better.
She really wants to have lots of energy to move around
and play with me.

Nonna had her operation, so now
I'm helping her. I walk with her
for 10 minutes everyday
so she can get better.

My nonna is my warrior.
She protects me from the world.

At 7:00 p.m, it's bath time. I've got to start getting ready for bed.

22

Nonna reads me a story every night before bedtime. I love this time.

I hear her as I'm falling asleep.
Nonna whispers "Sweet dreams!"
I know I am loved. Good night!

-end-

"With fewer than 50% of American households comprised of traditional families, there is a demand for non-traditional characters, stories, and role models."

2.9 million grandparents are raising over 4.5 million children in the United States, which means there are many children like Maddox. He wanted to share his story in **"A day in the life of an ordinary boy, Maddox".**

Author, Lynette Spano
Co-Author, Maddox Karpeshov

9 781513 644639